ARMY RANGERS

ASHLEY GISH

NORTH
AMERICA

SOUTH
AMERICA

EUROPE

AFRICA

ASIA

AUSTRALIA

T0018865

CREATIVE EDUCATION · CREATIVE PAPERBACKS

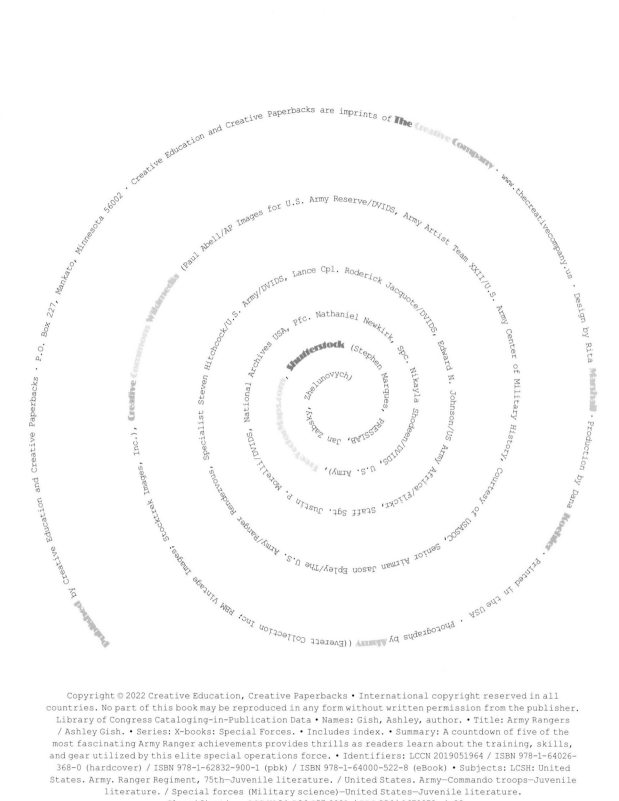

Published by Creative Education and Creative Paperbacks · P.O. Box 227, Mankato, Minnesota 56002 · Creative Education and Creative Paperbacks are imprints of The Creative Company · www.thecreativecompany.us · Design by Rita Marshall · Production by Dana Kochta · Printed in the USA · Photographs by Alamy ((Everett Collection Inc; RBM Vintage Images; Stocktrek Images, Inc.), Creative Commons Wikimedia (Paul Abell/AP Images for U.S. Army Reserve/DVIDS, Army Artist Team XXII/U.S. Army Center of Military History, Courtesy of USASOC, Senior Airman Jason Epley/The U.S. Army/Ranger Rendezvous, Specialist Steven Hitchcock/U.S. Army/DVIDS, National Archives USA, Pfc. Nathaniel Newkirk, Spc. Nikayla Shodeen/DVIDS, Lance Cpl. Roderick Jacquote/DVIDS, Edward N. Johnson/US Army Africa/Flickr, Staff Sgt. Justin P. Morelli/DVIDS, U.S. Army), PRESSLAB, Jan Zabsky, Shutterstock (Stephen Marques, Zhelunovych)

Library of Congress Cataloging-in-Publication Data • Names: Gish, Ashley, author. • Title: Army Rangers / Ashley Gish. • Series: X-books: Special Forces. • Includes index. • Summary: A countdown of five of the most fascinating Army Ranger achievements provides thrills as readers learn about the training, skills, and gear utilized by this elite special operations force. • Identifiers: LCCN 2019051964 / ISBN 978-1-64026-368-0 (hardcover) / ISBN 978-1-62832-900-1 (pbk) / ISBN 978-1-64000-522-8 (eBook) • Subjects: LCSH: United States. Army. Ranger Regiment, 75th—Juvenile literature. / United States. Army—Commando troops—Juvenile literature. / Special forces (Military science)—United States—Juvenile literature.
Classification: LCC UA34.R36 G57 2021 / DDC 356/.1670973—dc23
CCSS: RI.3.1–8; RI.4.1–5, 7; RI.5.1–3, 8; RI.6.1–2, 4, 7; RH.6-8.3-8

First Edition HC 9 8 7 6 5 4 3 2 1 • First Edition PBK 9 8 7 6 5 4 3 2 1

ARMY RANGERS

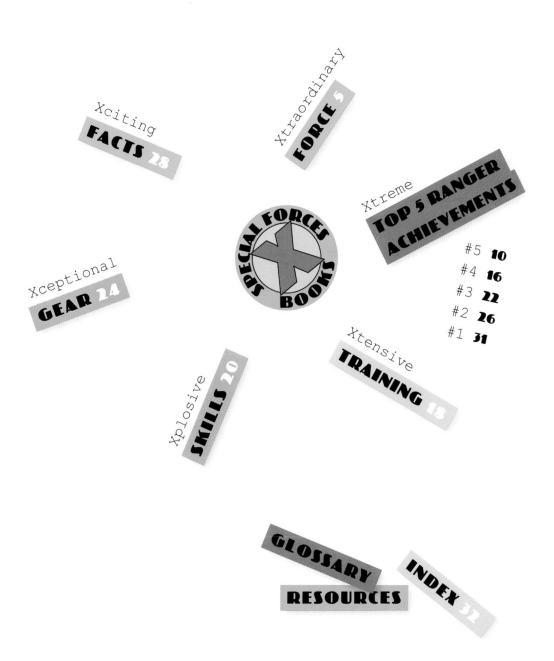

U.S. ARMY OFFICER RANKS

SECOND LIEUTENANT
FIRST LIEUTENANT
CAPTAIN
MAJOR
LIEUTENANT COLONEL
COLONEL
BRIGADIER GENERAL
MAJOR GENERAL
LIEUTENANT GENERAL
GENERAL
GENERAL OF THE ARMY

XTRAORDINARY FORCE

United States Army Rangers are fit, tough, and honorable. Army Rangers work on dangerous military missions. They use speed and force in challenging situations.

Ranger Basics

Army Rangers make up the 75th Ranger Regiment. It is one of the U.S. Army's special operations forces. The regiment is separated into five teams, called battalions.

Rangers specialize in direct-action missions. These are fast, short assaults. They often involve close combat and direct fire. Many occur deep into enemy territory. Missions may include taking or destroying enemy materials. Others involve rescuing—or taking—hostages. Rangers can carry out airborne attacks. They may take over enemy airfields or other key locations.

RANGER BATTALIONS

The 75th Ranger Regiment is always ready for combat. Ranger battalions can arrive at target locations within 18 hours of getting an order.

2ND BATTALION

Fort Lewis, Washington

UNITED STATES OF AMERICA

GEORGIA

1st BATTALION

Hunter Army Airfield

Hinesville, Georgia

GEORGIA

3rd BATTALION

Fort Benning, Georgia

REGIMENTAL SPECIAL TROOPS BATTALION

Fort Benning, Georgia

REGIMENTAL MILITARY INTELLIGENCE BATTALION

Fort Benning, Georgia

Army Rangers focus on the "big five" during training and missions. These are small-unit tactics, mobility, marksmanship, medical training, and physical training.

BIG FIVE
FOCUS

Not everyone can become a Ranger. People who want to become Rangers must be in the military. They must also be U.S. citizens. To qualify for Ranger training, soldiers must be physically and mentally fit. They cannot have any physical limitations. They must meet certain scores on a variety of tests.

Most Ranger missions remain classified.

TOP-SECRET
X
MISSIONS

Each Ranger battalion is made up of two to four companies.

TOP FIVE XTREME RANGER ACHIEVEMENTS

Xtreme Ranger Achievement #5

Ranger School In 2015, Kristen Griest and Shaye Haver became the first women to graduate Ranger School. Before completing the leadership course, Griest served in the military police. Haver was an attack helicopter pilot. Despite earning their Ranger tab, neither woman could continue Ranger training. At the time, female soldiers were not allowed in combat roles. Since 2015, several more women have successfully completed Ranger School.

Soldiers from any military branch can attend Ranger School.

Upon graduating, they receive a Ranger tab decoration.

Ranger Beginnings

Soldiers with Ranger-like skills have fought for centuries. In the early 1600s, European settlers scrambled to defend themselves against American Indian attacks. Some men began traveling long distances while looking for signs of danger. The skills they developed became the basis for soldiers called rangers.

The first ranger units were formed during the French and Indian War (1754-63). The most famous was Rogers' Rangers. Major Robert Rogers taught his men "Rules of Ranging." This guide was made up of 28 tactics he had learned from **allies** and enemies alike. After the war, Rogers' Rangers disbanded. But they fought again in the Revolutionary War (1775-83). Both the Union and the Confederacy had ranging units during the Civil War (1861-65).

Rangers played a significant role in World War II (1939-45). They formed highly mobile fast-striking units. Their skills were needed again during the conflicts in Korea and Vietnam. Rangers have been in continuous service since the 1960s. In 1974, the 75th Ranger Regiment was formally established.

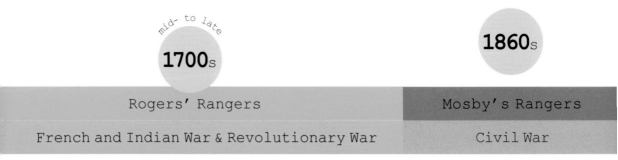

mid- to late **1700s**

1860s

Rogers' Rangers	Mosby's Rangers
French and Indian War & Revolutionary War	Civil War

1960s to 1970s

2000s

Lurps

1st, 2nd, & 3rd Battalions

Vietnam War

Operation Enduring Freedom

RANGER BEGINNINGS FACT

Robert Rogers offered to fight for America in the Revolutionary War.

But he was turned down. So Rogers' Rangers fought for the British.

TOP FIVE XTREME RANGER ACHIEVEMENTS

Xtreme Ranger
Achievement #4

Rangers Lead the Way! Lieutenant Colonel William Darby (pictured) was put in charge of the newly formed Ranger units at the start of World War II. He taught his men the original "Rules of Ranging." During the Normandy invasion on June 6, 1944, Allied soldiers were pinned down by German forces. Brigadier General Norman Cota rushed into battle. He shouted, "Rangers lead the way!" With the Rangers' help, the attack was successful.

XTENSIVE TRAINING

Soldiers who want to join the 75th Ranger Regiment must pass the Ranger Assessment and Selection Program (RASP). RASP lasts only eight weeks. It is extremely challenging, both mentally and physically.

LIFE AS A TRAINEE FACT

Experienced officers go through RASP 2. The course lasts just three weeks, but it is every bit as challenging and educational as RASP.

RASP graduation rate

33%

67%

pass

fail

Candidates are required to complete "Jump School."

AIRBORNE SCHOOL

Life as a Trainee

Candidates must meet certain standards to begin RASP training. Those who qualify enter Phase 1 of the course. This stage teaches the importance of teamwork. In Phase 1, trainees are constantly tested. They get little rest. They are quizzed on Ranger history and traditions. Trainees learn to find target locations using only a map and a compass. They march for miles carrying hundreds of pounds of gear. Unexpected obstacles are added to further challenge them. They are forced to make quick decisions. Instructors watch to see how candidates respond to stress.

In Phase 2, the focus shifts to hands-on skills. Candidates are trained to use a variety of weapons. They learn how to drive assault vehicles and use explosives. They are also taught how to plan and carry out direct-action missions.

Rangers are also expected to attend Ranger School. This 61-day program focuses on small-unit leadership. It teaches valuable skills for high-stress situations.

XPLOSIVE SKILLS

Training for the 75th Ranger Regiment is short compared to other special forces units. Additional courses sharpen Rangers' skills. Many train to fill specific roles. Then they work together as a team.

Ranger platoons are made up of about 30 troops. Each platoon has squads of seven to nine men, as well as a medic, radio operator, and forward observer.

Army Rangers are known for their ability to blend in with their surroundings. They are good at remaining undetected in enemy territory. Some are snipers. They can shoot targets more than 1,000 yards (914 m) away.

Medics have additional first-aid training. They treat injured soldiers. Some Rangers work with multipurpose canines. These dogs are trained to sniff out explosives and other dangers. They protect soldiers.

Joint fire support specialists provide important support to other Rangers. They set up and maintain communications systems. They can create secret coded messages. They can also decode enemy messages.

3

@

#

!

★ Xtreme Ranger Achievement #3

Canine Ranger Maiko was a multipurpose canine. He was put through the Advanced Handler's Course at Fort Benning. Afterwards, he was assigned to the 75th Ranger Regiment's 2nd Battalion. Maiko was deployed six times. He went on more than 50 raids. In November 2018, Maiko led Rangers into a building in Afghanistan. He was killed by enemy fire. But his actions saved the lives of his handler and other Rangers.

XCEPTIONAL GEAR

On missions, Rangers rely on a wide range of gear and weapons. They use everything from shotguns to missile launchers. Helmets, gloves, and body armor help keep them safe.

Ranger Gear

A Ranger's standard weapon is a light, automatic rifle. Strips of metal on the sides, called side rails, allow soldiers to add equipment to their guns. Rangers may attach a scope or a grenade launcher to their gun's side rails. Shotguns can be used to force open locked doors. One shot to the lock is all it takes to pop a door open.

Some Rangers use an M3 Carl Gustav. This gun fires explosive, smoke, and illumination rounds. Explosive rounds destroy tanks. Smoke rounds hide troops from enemies. Illumination rounds reveal the location of enemies in total darkness.

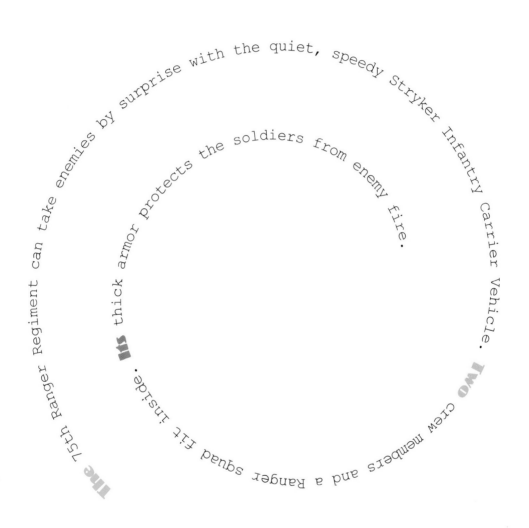

Ranger gear is strapped on with

Velcro and secured with duct tape.

The 75th Ranger Regiment can take enemies by surprise with the quiet, speedy Stryker Infantry Carrier Vehicle. Two crew members and a Ranger squad fit inside. Its thick armor protects the soldiers from enemy fire.

lightweight, custom-made gear.

Xtreme Ranger Achievement #2

Merrill's Marauders General Frank Merrill led Rangers through jungles in the South Pacific during World War II. The men marched more than 1,000 miles (1,609 km) in six months. They often lacked food, water, and sleep. Many fell ill with tropical diseases. Still, these Rangers fought enemy units much larger than their own. Their final battle occurred in August 1944. Every member of Merrill's Marauders received a **Bronze Star** after the victory.

During the Korean War, Rangers were used for secret information-gathering missions.

Robert Rogers paid his Rangers with his own money when governments could not afford to.

It takes one person to load an M3 Carl Gustav and another person to fire it.

Deployed Rangers cut up plastic water bottles so enemies cannot reuse them.

Graduating from Ranger School does not gain entry to the elite 75th Ranger Regiment.

More than half of all students fail Ranger School because it is so demanding.

The original "Rules of Ranging" tell soldiers to be up before dawn.

Rangers must be able to jump from aircraft and land safely using a parachute.

Phase 1 of RASP is meant to weed out soldiers who are not mentally tough.

When deployed, Ranger battalions undertake more missions than regular army units.

The Regimental Special Troops Battalion focuses on communication and **intelligence**.

After successfully completing RASP, Rangers receive tan caps called berets.

The 75th Ranger Regiment is one of the few units

continuously in action since the War on Terror

began in 2001.

Xtreme Ranger
Achievement #1

Pointe du Hoc During World War II, the
U.S. planned to attack German forces on the
beaches of Normandy, France. But Allies
learned of German guns atop Pointe du Hoc.
This cliff overlooks the coast. The guns
could strike anyone coming ashore. Rangers
were sent to destroy the guns. They had to
climb the 100-foot (30.5 m) cliff. They
discovered the "guns" were just logs. Soon
after, the Rangers found and destroyed real
enemy weapons.

GLOSSARY

allies – states or governments cooperating with each other for a common purpose

Bronze Star – a medal given for heroic achievements in combat

intelligence – information about movements and strength of enemy forces

RESOURCES

Garstecki, Julia. *Army Rangers*. North Mankato, Minn.: Black Rabbit Books, 2019.

Kohl, Peter. *My Dad Is in the Army*. New York: PowerKids Press, 2016.

"United States Army Facts for Kids." Kiddle. https://kids.kiddle.co/United_States_Army.

INDEX

About 75 percent of Delta Force members start out with the 75th Ranger Regiment.